Life
on the Farm

Be Not Afraid

Children's Stories

Life on the Farm

Published by 1st World Publishing
P.O. Box 2211, Fairfield, Iowa 52556
tel: 641-209-5000 • fax: 866-440-5234
web: www.1stworldpublishing.com

First Edition

LCCN: 2013912029
ISBN: 978-1-4218-8672-5

This material has been written and published for educational purposes to enhance one's wellbeing. In regard to health issues, the information is not intended as a substitute for appropriate care and advice from health professionals, nor does it equate to the assumption of medical or any other form of liability on the part of the publisher or author. The publisher and author shall have neither liability nor responsibility to any person or entity with respect to loss, damages or injury claimed to be caused directly or indirectly by any information in this book.

Most of us know someone who has endured the suffering of a serious medical challenge. Both the fear and uncertainty of the challenge itself and its treatment can overwhelm one's soul.

This book is dedicated to all of the children who have ever had to deal with the fear of a serious medical challenge. Furthermore, it offers bold encouragement through their unique journey.

We offer a special thank you to our friend, Linda. She had a heartfelt passion for children's literacy. During her personal cancer journey she inspired these children's stories about faith and courage.

It is our hope that all who read our books will be inspired by the truth that God is with them at all times, and they should always...*Be Not Afraid.*

Isaiah 41:10

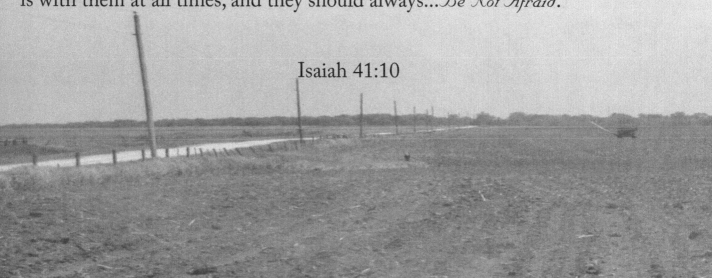

It is not easy being on the farm.
Each day starts very early.

Each day ends very late.

On the farm, everyone is part of the family.

And EVERYONE
has a name.

This bull is
Lawrence.

He has many
friends.

Their names are
Bootsy, Popeye,
and Clementine.

And for life on the farm, it takes a special kind of doctor
to keep everything healthy.

It takes a doctor to care for Lawrence, Bootsy, Popeye, Clementine,
and all of the farm friends.

It takes a doctor who makes house calls – well, farm calls.
It takes a doctor who wears boots. And a doctor who gets
muddy and who is ready to help around the farm.

It takes one that doesn't mind stepping
in smelly and squishy cow pies.
It takes a special kind of doctor.

And it takes a praying doctor – that's our Doc Woody.

Doc Woody is a veterinarian. A vet is a doctor who cares
for the farm animal family when one is sick or hurt.
Johnny likes Doc's gentle touch and his quiet prayer.

Johnny wants to feel better because he loves to let children ride around, around, and around.

It takes a wise doctor to know just when to
scratch and sooth Popeye's annoying itch, too.

Doc Woody understands that farmers work with BIG machines and that bad accidents can happen.

He prays for the farmers to be careful.

Doc likes to see
all things on the farm,
from livestock to grain,
grow and be healthy.

He asks God to watch over the sprouting corn in the fields.
It is small and can easily be hurt by storms and wind.

After many months, the corn will be done growing.
Then, it will be time to harvest it out of the field.

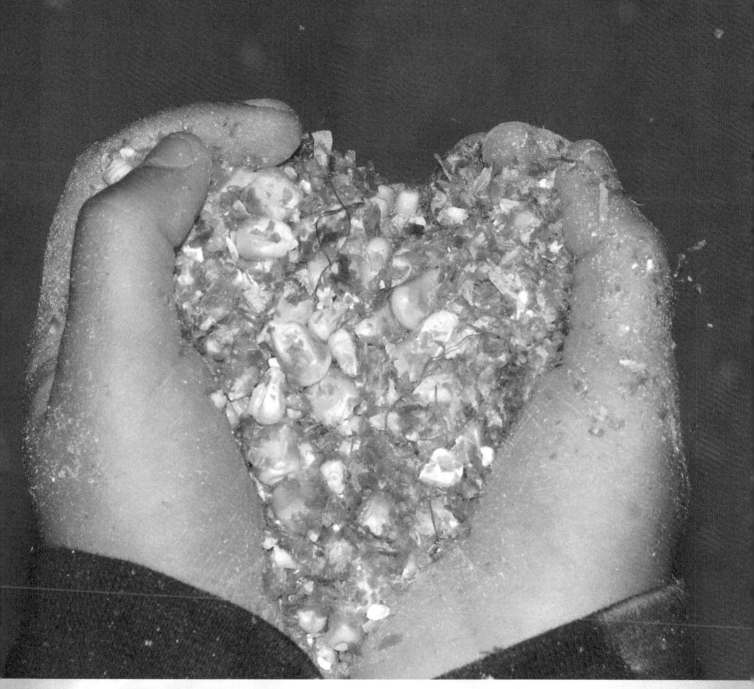

Corn will feed Lawrence, his friends, and the baby calves.
Corn will feed Johnny. This will make them grow and be healthy.
Doc Woody thanks God for the harvest.

Doc Woody always prays for the young farmers.

And he prays for their bigger and older brothers and sisters, too.

Life on the farm is filled with lots of work and lots of fun.
Farmers love life on the farm.

It is even more fun with Brady, your best friend.

Our Doc Woody is a special kind of doctor.
He is wise, compassionate, and encouraging.
He has a gentle-hand and a healing-touch.

During our muddy, stormy, squishy times
we need to pray to God for bravery and courage.

God watches over us, day and night,
just as Doc Woody watches over Lawrence, Johnny, Bootsy,
Popeye, Clementine, and others of the farm animal family.
May we always find our faith and courage in God through prayer.

Be Not Afraid children's stories were created to celebrate
a wise, loving, and faithful God.

When I am afraid, I put my trust in you.

—Psalm 56:3

Life On The Farm is a simple reality of a rural Iowa farm life with its smelly, squishy truths, and the need for daily farm prayer. You will get to know Lawrence, the bull, and Doc Woody, the vet, in this heartwarming story. This story reminds us of our need for divine strength during our muddy times of life.

Ozzie is happy dog and a great bedtime story. **Ozzie and His Brave Amen** is the story of a howling beagle. His care for others and climbing talent leads him on a wonderful adventure. Ozzie's bedtime story is shared with our children...and now with yours. It will make you smile and want to read it often.

He's Got My Whole World in His Hands...if this one doesn't make you giggle – check your pulse. Only innocent babies can understand God's love in its purity. They will share their God-filled perspective and make you smile. You will enjoy this one and feel good all day.

CPSIA information can be obtained at www.ICGtesting.com
Printed in the USA
LVOW01s0415151113

361129LV00001B/1/P